# THE BATTLE OF SIDI NSIR

A PERSONAL ACCOUNT

BY

PRIVATE JOHN ABRAHAM ABRAMIDES MM

# The Battle of Sidi Nsir

A Personal Account

By

Private John Abraham Abramides MM

For Babs

"Don't give up until you've used all your ammunition or you're dead."

"After 17.00 hours O.C. B Company reported that his strength was now about 30, that the enemy were closing in on him and that they were round behind his right or southern flank. No further report was received from this Company, and no single Officer or man came back."

"From eye-witness survivors and reports received by wireless during the action there is no doubt that this action was an epic which can seldom have been excelled for heroism and devotion to duty. All ranks fought magnificently and to the death."

*The Royal Hampshire Regiment Journal August, 1947*

"Contact with the enemy was made along the mountain ridges east of Sidi Nsir. A swampy spot in the road along rocky slopes had been infested with most carefully camouflaged mines so that the first Panzer going through had been immobilized and was blocking up the road. Heavy artillery and mortar fire started, excellently directed from many favourable observation posts in the mountains. Pz. Pioniere sent forward were unable to clear the minefield or to get the immobilized leading Panzer going again, because sheafs of fire coming from M.G.

coming mainly from the flanks, mowed down every single man."

*Battles of Lang in Tunisia (10th Panzer Division)*
*by Oberst. Rudolf Lang*

"Our failure at Sidi Nsir and Hunts Gap marked the end of our hopes of victory in North Africa".

*German Afrika Corps Commander*
*talking to Brigadier Graham after the war*

*Private John Abramides' account of the Battle of Sidi Nsir appeared in the summer 2011 edition of The Royal Hampshire Regiment Journal, Tiger Talk. He was a member of B Company of the 5th Hampshire Regiment which fought alongside C Company and 155 Battery (172nd Field Regiment Royal Artillery) at Sidi Nsir on the 26th February 1943. The following account of the battle was recorded by his grandson, in 2010.*

"The trouble is, you never know how you will react when you are in the battle situation. You do the training, firing blanks, but when you fire at someone and they go down, it makes your hair stand on end. We had a lance corporal with us, a big man - he was a heavyweight boxer. When the tanks appeared he turned to jelly and couldn't even get his cigarettes out to have a smoke. We got a cigarette for him. He could do nothing. He said he was okay with infantry but the tanks were different. They used to punish soldiers who couldn't fight - but that's wrong. If your nerve goes there's nothing you can do about it. When the time comes you can either turn to jelly like that or turn into a tiger and you just don't know beforehand how you will react"

*After defeat at the Second Battle of El Alamein, the Panzer Army Africa under Field Marshal Rommel had retreated into south-eastern Tunisia, becoming isolated from the German held port towns of Tunis and Bizerte in the north. Rommel's attempt to reverse the retreat, with a counter-offensive into central Tunisia, met with initial success. Supply bases at Faid and Sidi Bou Zid were taken, forcing an Allied retreat to Kasserine Pass where the famous and bloody battles began five days later. General Anderson, commanding the British 1st Army in* the north, had no alternative but to send reinforcements south in the shape of a tanks corps, leaving the northern forces vulnerable to attack.

Operation 'Ochsenkopf' ('Bull's Head') had been planned to regain the initiative in the north, by breaking through Allied lines to join with Rommel in the south. The main target was Béja, a key communications centre with important road and rail links, which held vital ordnance and food supplies. The capture of Béja was critical, and Sidi Nsir, a small hamlet in a valley on the road and rail-line to Béja, was to see the main thrust of the offensive - led by an armoured Battle Group including the 10th Panzer Division under the command of Colonel Lang, together with the new and much vaunted 'Tiger Tanks'.

The position at Sidi Nsir was held by territorial troops: one battalion of infantry, the 5th Hampshires, and one battery of artillery, 155 Battery (172nd Field

*Regiment Royal Artillery) armed with eight, 25-pounder gun howitzers. On the 26th February, Sidi Nsir became a focal point for the entire North Africa Campaign - the puncture point for Operation Ochsenkopf.*

*The troops at Sidi Nsir were charged with the duty of delaying the enemy, to give one extra day for the weakened position at Hunt's Gap – a tank run into Béja - to be reinforced.*

*Private John Abramides, of B Company of the 5th Hampshire Battalion, found himself in Sidi Nsir, Tunisia in February 1943. On the 26th February, having stood down for breakfast, he saw the first German tanks approaching. The following account was given 67 years later in August, 2010.*

When we stood down for breakfast I would always take my boots off and rest my feet before putting my other boots on. We had just stood down and I had undone my shoelaces. I was talking to the lance corporal in my Bren group. My number two, Burton, had taken some eggs to make an arrangement with the kitchen. I had suggested that he take the spare Bren barrel and working parts with him so he wouldn't have to come back to the trench. It wasn't long after he had gone that we saw the first tank appear.

My first reaction was to laugh and say, "I had better do up my laces. I may need to run."

The lance corporal said, "I don't know why you are laughing."

"What else can we do," I said, "cry?" That's when I turned to look at him and saw that he was white and shaking and his legs had gone.

It was early in the morning, about six-thirty I think, when the German tanks first appeared in the distance, coming round the bend in the road. Then we heard shelling and we rushed to our positions. In the days before, I had found a position partway up a hill overlooking the minefield across the road in the valley below. We had dug the trench behind a rock to give extra protection, but the ground was rocky so our trench was less than four foot deep. On the opposite hill there were Germans. To my left the road curved round the hill and on towards the railway station and our 25-pounders, but I could not see them from my trench. The hill went up behind me and there was also a hill to my right.

Burton had rushed back to join me in the trench and he hadn't had time to get the eggs cooked so we never got our breakfast and, although I didn't know it at the time, in the confusion the spare parts had been left behind as well.

Soon after we had word from Captain Lytle, the company commander. We were told we were not to withdraw, but to defend the minefield until late afternoon. The order was to stay until we were dead, or ran out of ammunition.

Once in the trench it wasn't long - probably less than half and hour - before the first tank, a Panzer, came into the valley. It reached several yards into the field before it hit a mine and blew up. A soldier came up looking dazed and I put my Bren on a single round and I said to Burton, "I'm going to get him in the heart." So I shot him. And if you would have been there, I'm sure my hair stood up because it felt like little needles sticking into my head. And I thought, "Christ, this is real. I had killed a man."

It wasn't long before we were joined in the trench by two others; one was an officer who was with the 25-pounders and the other, a sergeant with a radio. The officer had come forward to direct the fire of the 25-pounders; he was a tall man and struggled to fit in the trench. I had spent three or four days on reconnaissance with him in the days before the battle and I liked him. He used to ask for me - the soldier with the moustache - to accompany him to provide machine gun cover. Captain Lytle said I didn't have to go every time, but I found it interesting. During those days I learned how accurate the British gunners were. The 25-pounder guns had armour-piercing shells and I watched the gunners as they practised firing and the officer made notes. The idea was to zero the guns on certain targets during the day so they could go back at night to attack the German camps. The officer would have a map and he would radio instructions to the gunners to fire a shell in order to see how accurate he was. On one occasion he passed me some binoculars and asked me if I could see a tree with a marquee beneath it. He told me to keep my eye on the target. I did and saw a direct hit; the marquee exploded in front of my eyes. They were very accurate with those guns, but the German tanks, with their extra thick armour, later proved too much for them in the battle.

We didn't wait long before German soldiers with minesweepers came forward into the minefield. The officer started counting them... one... two... three... four... five... and I remember something about fourteen. He started pushing me. "Come on soldier, what do you think you're doing? When are you going to fire at them?" But I was waiting, wondering how many more would come, and I was taking aim and deciding where I would I get them. In the end I fired on the rear soldier in front of the first tank, and I kept my fire on that spot. And as I fired they ran back. I kept my fire steady and as they ran I was getting them. They were all just running back in a straight line because it was a mine field, and they ran back into my my line of fire, a lot of them, falling one on top of another. And some of them, they had a lot more bullets than one or two or three; they had more because they were falling in the direction of my fire. It was a massacre ... it was terrible.

Then the shelling started. The German tanks shelled again and again. They had 88mm guns on the tanks, and they shook the hill up. When a shell hit the rock underneath our position, your stomach went up into your mouth. My watch fell to pieces, the mechanism rattled inside. The same with the sergeant's radio. The vibration, it was terrible. And my helmet, I don't know what was hitting it, but every time something exploded, I would have to pick it up and put it back on again. When I looked at it afterwards it was bent and dented everywhere. I wish I could have brought it back, nobody would have believed that the person wearing it could have survived.

The officer then told me to ceasefire and we started arguing. "I can't do that, sir. My orders are to stay here until I'm dead or I've got no ammunition." He told me his guns were good, and to leave the fight to them, but I told him his guns wouldn't stand against the German tanks once they were through the minefield. He even threatened to court martial me. "Haven't you been told to obey the last officer's orders?" he asked.

I had been told that, but this was different, "You're with the 25-pounders. Me, I'm infantry."

I asked Burton for the spare barrel as my Bren was getting hot, and that's when I discovered he'd left it behind. So what could we do? We couldn't keep firing. You've got to cease fire, if you like it or not, otherwise, you will have no gun. So the four of us crouched in the trench as shell after shell came down, looking when we could, and waiting for the Bren to cool down.

The officer was hit in the head, probably by some shrapnel, and the wound was bleeding badly. I used my field dressing, but he told me to use his instead. In the end I used both dressings and still there was blood everywhere. I remember saying, "Now look sir, I'm sorry about all this but if you want to go out and see the MO, you follow me and I'll take you out."

"No," he said, "I'm staying now."

Some time later the shelling stopped. With my watch broken, I had no idea of the time. I saw an officer; he looked like the tank commander, sitting in a Panzer looking around with his binoculars. "I'm going to have him," I thought. My Bren was beginning to cool down and I shot him. Then the guns opened up again, all the guns seemed to line up on on our position. The earth was shaking, and then the machine guns started as well, spraying the ground up with bullets, filling our trench with soil. I thought, this is our end.

But for all the shells and all the bullets we survived. We were lucky. At one point a Panzer gun was pointed straight at us and I remember trying to put some shot into the barrel, but it was useless to even try.

All the time the thing we feared most was that any minute we were going to get a grenade in the trench. Another gunner further up the hill was covering our position. In the previous days I had told him that I was relying on him to cover my back. We were expected to make arrangements like that, working as a team. So I called out to him, asked him to look out for German soldiers coming up behind us. He called back, "I can't see anything from here but

I'll go and have a look." It was the first time we had communicated that day.

A little while later he shouted back. "Oh Christ, John, they're on top of you," he said, "and I haven't brought my rifle." Almost immediately the guns stopped firing and I knew the Germans had to be close. I stood up in the trench with my gun in my hand and I saw three of them. I opened up the Bren. They were so close one of them rolled down right to the edge of our trench.

I told the others to get out quickly, and they went, the officer, the sergeant and Burton. Later I discovered that the injured officer reported me to my company commander, Captain Lytle. The gunnery officer wanted me disciplined or imprisoned for disorder. The radio operator told me about it afterwards. In response, Lytle suggested the officer should hurry back and see the MO to get his wound dressed.

So I stopped there on my own. I couldn't tell you how long I was there, but it seemed like hours. During that time a German plane came over and it was so low I could see the pilot. I turned my Bren to take aim, and with the plane so low I barely had to lift the barrel. As I fired, the tracers seemed to show that I was on target to hit the pilot. The plane crashed into the hill opposite. I don't know if it was anything to do with me or whether an anti-aircraft gun hit the plane.

Can you imagine how relieved I was when Captain Lytle called me over? I'd been on my own in the trench and it had been quiet for a long time. I couldn't see what was going on so

I was just waiting for something to happen. Waiting for a grenade to come into the trench. I was certain they would get me.

I later discovered that the German officer didn't want to needlessly sacrifice his men to capture my machine gun and so he used the captured British soldiers to persuade me to surrender. They called down to me, telling me to surrender. I didn't want to surrender because we had been told to hold the Germans until late afternoon, and I also thought there would be someone waiting to shoot me.

Finally the wireless operator of my commanding officer came under cover to the ridge of the hill and called me. He said, "John, come back. Captain Lytle said you have to come back." So I dragged my Bren and the ammunition I had left and, keeping down, went round the hill to where Captain Lytle and his wireless operator were behind a rock on a flat piece of ground partway up the hill. It was a place I had previously used for sleeping. From this position I could no longer see the minefield or the tanks, but I could see the railway station and the 25-pounders.

There were some Germans with rifles nearby. I said to Captain Lytle, "Shall we try to get a few more?" I put my head round one side of the rock but they were ready for me. A bullet whistled past my ear. I then went to the other side and looked again. A bullet whistled past my other ear. Those bullets were so close I could feel the heat from them. I realised there was nothing we could do.

A British soldier who had been captured called down to me to surrender. I answered him and gave away my position. The Germans would have known then that I was no longer covering the minefield.

Captain Lytle said, "Abramides, there are only three of us left. I think you'd better give yourself up." The wireless operator went, but I hesitated. It was late in the afternoon and we had done what we were asked to do but I didn't know how the Germans would react to me if I surrendered - I had killed so many men.

I suggested to Lytle that we go together, but he refused. I told him, "I don't like this." And he nodded, but said, "Now look here. You live and fight again. That's my motto."

Again, a British soldier called out to me to surrender. I called out, "Are you sure they are not going to... I'm sure they want to kill me."

"They've promised they won't kill you," he said. "They're not going to fire - you just come out."

Just before I surrendered I saw the tanks coming round the hill to face the 25-pounders. I could see and hear the shells of the 25-pounders ricocheting off the tanks and whistling up in the air. They didn't stand a chance against those tanks. I only saw one tank damaged; its turret had been shifted. The battle was soon over and it was a terrible waste of life.

"All right, tell them I'm ready," I said, and stepped forward. As soon as I put my hands up I saw a German officer coming down towards me. I thought, "Blimey," but he came down towards me and said in English, "Were you the machine gunner there?"

"Yes, sir." I answered, and he patted me on the back. "Good soldier, good soldier," he said, "that's how I like soldiers to be."

Can you imagine? I think if I had been a German they would have given me the iron cross right there and then. He walked down to the trench where I had been and he had a look at it. I didn't like to ask, though, if I could collect my spare boots, money and chocolate. Then as we walked up the hill we talked.

"Before I came to this front I was on the Russian front, he told me. "I don't call them soldiers because they aren't soldiers. They gave their lives away; fifty so-called soldiers gave their lives away for one of my machine guns. That's not soldiering. If you and the Americans help them win the war you will regret it."

He asked me if I knew anyone from Bristol, and I remember saying, "No, they come from everywhere else." I asked him if he had any relatives there, but he said, "No, I was at the University before the war, and I knew a girl there."

I had gained some confidence by then and I was hungry; we'd missed breakfast and I'd had nothing all day. "You've got a lot of boxes there, sir," I said. "Is there any chance you could open them?"

When we had captured German soldiers, on patrol in the days before the battle, we had given them some food or chocolate - to reassure them that they were going to be all right. The Germans who captured us behaved in the same way.

The officer said, "Get them in line and I'll get someone to open them." The boxes were opened and the packets were handed out. And what did I get? Just coffee and sugar.

Later I saw a German soldier eating and I asked if I could have some. He broke his food into two and gave me half. Another handed over his water bottle.

Of the captured British soldiers, a lance corporal spoke to me first. "John, I'm glad to see you," he said. "I didn't think I would see you alive again." He told me that the German officer had told him, *"You've got a very good gunner there, but we're going to kill him."*

Shortly after I was captured it started to get dark and it was raining. I was exhausted but through the night we began the long walk to the port - Bizerte or Tunis, I'm not sure - where we were to be put on a boat for Italy.

I sometimes think I may have let Captain Lytle down when I delayed surrendering. He didn't tell me that he was planning to escape. The radio operator had surrendered but I took my time. I wanted Captain Lytle to come with me. He should have told me what his plans were but he didn't. I took my time and I think Captain Lytle was waiting to see me surrender. Perhaps if he had gone straight away, he would have got away. But by the time he went down to the driver of the Bren carrier, the tanks were across the minefield and already overcoming the 25-pounders. I think the driver was shot in the hand and both he and Captain Lytle were captured.

Following his capture at Sidi Nsir, Private Abramides was transported to a prisoner of war camp in Capua, Italy. He remained there until June 1943 when he was transferred to Campo 53 in Macerata. After the Armistice with Italy, the camp was taken over by German soldiers, who prepared to take the prisoners of war to Germany. Private Abramides was entrained on 19th September. Under cover of darkness, he jumped out of the moving train with two other prisoners of war and they made their way south, back towards the Allied lines.

Private Abramides was recaptured on 22nd October, but with an Italian ID card, he was able to pass as an Italian and was released. He finally crossed the German front near Vasto and entered the British camp on the 4th November. He was transported to Termoli *and then Taranto.  Eventually he was taken to Algiers before being put on a boat for England.*

## Post Script

On the boat coming home I met a Major who was at Hunt's Gap with the tank corps. He was returning to England to prepare for the second front. A Captain had said that they wanted a hairdresser and barber. I didn't think I would be able to do it because I was feeling weak and didn't think I could stand long enough, but I was persuaded to try and I helped another barber, a Scotsman, and earned about £20 in five days. One day the Major wanted a haircut and as I was cutting his hair we talked. I told him I was in the Hampshire regiment.

As I was brushing him down afterwards he asked which battalion I was in, and I told him I was in the 5th. Immediately he embraced me and said, "Ah, the 5th Hampshires … a fine battalion, the best battalion in the British army." I told him that I was the Bren gunner who defended the minefield and he was delighted. He explained that he had arrived at Hunt's Gap with time to get his tanks and guns, including a 17-pounder, in position. He said that the guns were dug in low down beside the road. He then told his men to eat their rations and then rest until the Germans came. They were told not to fire until he gave the order, because he wanted the Germans to get close.

The 17-pounder gunners were ordered to focus all their fire on the Tiger tanks.

"In a few days," he said, "we were back holding your positions at Sidi Nsir."

# After the Battle of Sidi Nsir:

# An Escape Through Italy

A PERSONAL ACCOUNT

BY

Private John Abraham Abramides MM

"The Germans were in the next carriage and I knew I had to act fast. As soon as I'd got the door open, Larry went. Then Mick made his way through to me. He gave me my tunic and bag and he was off as well. I pulled on my tunic, not stopping to button the cuffs. It crossed my mind that the Germans might have caught sight of the others and have their guns ready. But I didn't want the train to take me too far from Larry and Mick, so I held on to the side of the carriage with both hands, lowered myself as far as possible, and twisting forward, jumped into the

darkness."


*Private John Abramides' account of the Battle of Sidi Nsir appeared in the summer 2011 edition of The Royal*

*Hampshire Regiment Journal, Tiger Talk. He was a member of B Company of the 5th Hampshire Regiment which fought alongside C Company and 155 Battery (172nd Field Regiment Royal Artillery) at Sidi Nsir on the 26th February 1943. On the evening of the battle, he was captured and eventually transported to a prisoner of war camp in Capua, Italy. The following account of his escape was given 71 years later in February, 2014.*

After I surrendered, the battle was soon over and we were taken to the road, which was on lower ground. The Germans wanted to move all of us together so we were herded up awaiting the last of the prisoners. A mate of mine, Mickey Walker, gave me a piece of chocolate because I was so hungry. It was a type that was meant to be taken with water so it would swell up and keep hunger at bay. Unfortunately, I had no water. While we were waiting, I remember lying on my back trying to catch drops of rain in my mouth. I regretted leaving my water and chocolate in the trench, not to mention my new boots, which would have been a real asset to me later on.

We were eventually led away, not really knowing where we were heading. We didn't stop to sleep but just kept walking through the night and through the next day. The night before the battle had been very tense and I had been woken several times so hadn't had much rest. Then a day in the trench—without any food and with the added tension of the battle—left me in a bad way, and I was falling asleep as I walked. On one occasion I almost hit the ground before I woke up. On the journey I saw another prisoner who was struggling and I asked him what the problem was.  He was one of the gunners and he said that a tank had driven over the trench he was in.  "The b******s turned the tank round deliberately and I hurt my back."

He was one of the small number of gunners who survived once the tanks got through the minefield.  There was no way they could defeat tanks because they were so exposed and they shouldn't have been left in that position.  I'm sure they probably killed a number of Germans with their shells but in close combat with tanks, the situation was hopeless.  They should have been told to withdraw or surrender when it was clear they had no chance.  After all, by then it was late afternoon and the Germans had been held up for long enough.  To me, as a soldier, I thought it was a waste of life.

Eventually we reached a port but I don't

remember much about it. I wasn't sure whether we were in Tunis or Bizerte. We were given some food then, but I felt so ill at the time I remember very little.

Before we left for Italy I saw Mickey again. He told me that he and Captain Lytle had managed to get back to our old positions at Sidi Nsir without too much bother, even passing some Germans in the dark. But then they made the big mistake of asking an Arab for water. The Arab gave them some water but also turned them in to some Germans nearby. The pair were recaptured and taken by truck to the port. I remember also that Mickey had a pen, given to him by his wife so that he could write to her whilst he was away. He asked me to look after it for him so that he was not tempted to exchange it for food.

## Italy

We were taken by sea to Italy. The Germans put us straight into a hold on a ship—it was all metal—and they left us in there, shut in, until we got to Naples. We had no food or water on the journey and there were no toilets. Fortunately the journey was not long, just a day or so. We sat around and I remember, in one case, somebody had a cigarette, which they lit and passed round. In the end they had it on a matchstick to get the last puff out of it.

When we got to Naples, some of the chaps were very weak and had a bit of difficulty climbing up the metal steps of a vertical ladder that went straight up from the hold. I did struggle a bit, but I managed better than some. Once off the boat we were marched through Naples and then on to a camp at Capua in the shadow of

Vesuvius.

The guards who dealt with us were Italian soldiers. They looked dirty and pathetic. Their trousers were patched and they had no socks, just a bit of rag wrapped around their feet. It was terrible, terrible to look at them. They had less than we did. Their rifles were practically rusty. They looked like something from the time of Nelson.

I hated being in the prison camp and was determined from the very beginning to escape. Before the battle, we'd talked about dying, and wondered if it hurt when you got shot, but I'd never thought about being captured. From the very beginning I felt humiliated, that getting captured was a terrible thing. Some of the others were quite happy and pleased to have survived, but I just wanted to get away. There was no way that I could have waited it out until the end of the war. I was never really happy as a prisoner, not for one day. I always had to be doing something to stop myself from going mad. I could send letters and I wrote regularly to my parents. My father would write back, telling me to be diplomatic and not lose my temper.

One morning, I was told by other prisoners to be careful, because I was grinding my teeth in my sleep. Apparently as I did it, I was threatening the Italians, calling them you so-and-sos and telling them I would "put them in bundles of ten".

In the camp I met a soldier that I had trained with in England. He asked me if I remembered a lance corporal who used to stand on top of the trench to give us orders when we were training.

"It happened just as you told him it would," the soldier said, "He was killed just as you said."

I'd said to the lance corporal, "Now look here, Corporal, if you don't get down here with us and learn how to behave and you get over to the fighting, they'll knock your head off." Apparently he was shot in the head and killed because he stuck his head above the trench to answer someone who called out to him. It just shows how important it is to get into good habits when you are training.

We didn't have much in prison. We were given a few lire to buy things like toothbrushes, toothpaste, razors and razor blades. I assume the money was provided by the British government.

We discussed trying to escape but didn't think

we would get very far. There was a rumour that some prisoners had escaped but had been recaptured by the Italians. The Italians were going to shoot them but were stopped by some Germans soldiers on exercises in the camp. I did get talking to the Italian guards though, and I told them I was interested in the history of Italy and asked if they had any books about it. I was given a book which I held onto for a couple of days before returning it, asking if they had another I could borrow. By the third book I found what I was looking for—a map of Italy. I traced the map and hid it carefully before returning the book. This was the first step in my plan to escape and I still have the map today (See figure 1).

Life was tedious in the camp. There was little to do and no facilities for showering. We were allowed to run around a field at certain times and play football if we had a ball. A few of us would try to keep fit by doing some exercises with a Sergeant who had been a boxer. He was in charge of the kitchen and he would give us extra food at times. We would also go and talk through the fence to the black prisoners who were separated from us. They would say that they were fighting on the same side as us, in the same army, and didn't understand why they were segregated from us. We didn't know either; it must have been a decision of the Italian army.

Working in the camp was a Greek fellow who lived in Italy. He wasn't actually in the army but he was working as an interpreter for the Italians. He discovered my name and came to see me. He would speak to me in Greek and seemed friendly enough. He found out that I was a hairdresser and he asked me if I would cut hair and he'd give me some extra food. I did this for quite a while and I cut the hair of several prisoners. The Greek would bring in the tools when I needed them and then take them away again. I don't remember much about the food in the first camp but I must have been fairly satisfied with it because I remember the food in our next camp only too well.

At one time we had notices to go up for a working party. My name came up as well as my mate Mickey Walker's. When it came to the time to leave on the train, I found the names were to be called in alphabetical order. And because the Greek was the one calling out the names, I said to him, "Leave my name until you call Mickey Walker, and then call me because I'd like to go with him." We wanted to stay together in case there was a chance of escaping. I thought he'd agreed so I went off to the toilets and when I came back and Mickey Walker's name was called, I followed. The Greek immediately told the Italians that I should have been in a different compartment, so I was moved. I was angry, but I don't think there would have been much chance of getting away on that journey.

It turned out that we were not going on a working party after all, but were being moved to a different camp, in Macerata. I think perhaps that Capua was just a transit camp. It was sited close to a port and there was not much there. I'm not sure how long we were at Capua, but I think it was a few weeks rather than months, and the move to Macerata came as an unwelcome change.

## Macerata

Macerata was a much bigger camp. I think there were about seven and a half thousand people there. It was more secure than Capua with two barbed wire fences around the perimeter and searchlights that would sweep the camp all night. Guards were on duty in observation boxes throughout the night as well. Life was pretty grim there. Our diet revolved around pasta, rice, cabbage and onions. We would have pasta with onions one day, followed by pasta with cabbage the next; then it would be rice with onions and then rice with cabbage. This was accompanied by a small bread roll made with flour from ground corn. From time to time we would get Red Cross parcels, with tins of Nestlé's milk, porridge and Cadbury's chocolate.

In the camp there was a huge hole in the ground,

like a big chalk-hole, and above that there was a field where we could run. We could go there about 6 o'clock in the morning. The problem was that the hole was used by the Italians to dump rubbish. Every so often they would change the straw in their bedding and the old straw would go straight in the hole. Also dumped there were the empty Red Cross tins, which were never washed out. Consequently the place was full of fleas and flies. This made things unpleasant when I did a run around the field; after every lap I had to stop because my legs would be black with the fleas on them. It wasn't a question of picking the fleas off; I would have to brush them off before running again. And I could never dare wear socks because fleas would get into them and eat at my feet. I would scratch so much that my feet bled.

So for running, I would wear just a pair of trousers and run barefoot.

I remember one day I got a tin of tea—we would use the empty Red Cross tins as cups—and as I walked away something bit me at my waist. And it was so painful, I dropped the cup. When I looked down there was a body louse attached to me, sucking my blood. I brushed it away but where it had been there was a red blistered area. That was my first experience of a body louse, but it wouldn't be my last. We also had trouble with bugs at night. With double bunks for sleeping; I slept in a lower bunk and an RAF sergeant, a pilot, was in the top one. He had a leg wound as a result of parachuting from his plane. At night I would lie there half awake, with bed bugs dropping onto my face.

By now it was the height of summer, and I was

desperate for a shower. But there were so many of us in the camp and the water was turned on for only a very short time each day. There would be so many of us crammed into the washroom and even if you managed to get in sometimes the Italians would switch off the water before you could soap yourself. It was impossible to keep clean. Every day I would hope for something to happen, anything that could give us a chance to escape.

I first met Larry in Macerata. He was a PT instructor and he would go through some exercises with a few of the prisoners. I went along each day and he would give me exercises to strengthen my arms and shoulders. He gave me something to use as weights. The RAF sergeant would come along and give me encouragement. Referring to my shoulder and arm muscles, he would say, "Yeah, yeah, they're coming up." One day the sergeant caught Mick and me putting tins of Nestlé's milk, chocolate and porridge in a bag under my bed, and he asked if we were thinking of escaping. "The first chance I get, I'll be off," I told him, and hearing this, he gave me a little compass. "It'll never be any good to me." he said. "I'll never be able to use it with my leg, so you can have it." Just like the map I traced, I still have the compass to this day (see Figure 2). So now I had my map, a compass and a growing collection of food. When the opportunity arose, I would be ready to go.

If we were ever sick in the camp there was a doctor we could visit. I found out from some prisoners who reported sick that officers were kept separated from us in another part of the camp quite close to the sick bay. Mick and I wondered if Captain Lytle was there so we decided to investigate. We set off with the sick party one morning, pretending to be sick, and approached the officers' camp. We asked through the fence if anyone knew Captain Lytle. He was there and came to the fence to talk to us. Thereafter, we would go there occasionally to talk to him. We told him about our plans to escape and he said that he was planning to escape also. He and Mick exchanged addresses so that if we got back first we could write to his wife and if he got back before we did, he would write to Mickey's wife and my fiancée.

All the time we were in the camp at Macerata, escape seemed unlikely. There were look-out posts, lights and wires. And we were warned that we'd be shot if we crossed the wires. The only real chance was to wait to be taken out. But escape was on my mind all the time. I had no doubt that the Allies would eventually win the war, but I thought it might take years for the war to end. And for me a month in prison was a long time.

## Escape

Then one morning we heard shots fired, and were surprised to discover that our Italian guards had gone, and had been replaced by Germans. I don't know whether the Italians left or whether they surrendered, but we never saw them again. There had been no warning of this but it soon became clear that our new guards were preparing to take us to Germany by train. At last it seemed we might have an opportunity to escape. It was August by now so I had been a prisoner for nearly six months and there was no way that I wanted to spend any more time in a prison camp, especially in Germany. We were being put in groups of forty to be marched to the railway station. Several trains were needed as there were so many prisoners to transport. Mick and I decided that we would hang back so we would be among the last to go, and it was a couple more days before we left. As we were marched to the station we passed some little alleys and one of my company said, "You know Johnny, if we run through there they wouldn't let the others stay here and chase us would they?" I just laughed and said, "Well you can try if you like, but I wouldn't underestimate the Germans. If I were there, with that Tommy gun, I'd be able to cut you down before you got to the barriers."

At the station the train was filled up from the front and each compartment padlocked. I suggested to Mick that try to stay behind so that we would end up in the last compartment and hopefully they would run out of padlocks. I also thought that it would be safer to escape from the back of the train as we'd be less likely to be seen. The idea worked; we ended up in the last compartment and I hung around by the door giving out the food rations so I could watch the door being secured. Instead of a padlock, the Germans used a length of wire, twisted several times and then cut through so that the ends were almost welded together. As soon as the train set off, I set to work trying to open the door by working on the wire. The only tool I had was a piece of pipe I'd found in the camp. I think it was lead because it was very soft and I had beaten it with a stone until it was flattened like a knife. I found it impossible to untwist the wire and so I tried bending the wire backwards and forwards. This had no effect at all, so my only option was cut through.

All the while I was doing this, I was harassed by some others in the compartment. Some were mocking and another was saying, "Come on, give it up. Give it up; you've done your bit." But there was one who really annoyed me. He was in my way at the beginning, preventing me from getting close to the door. I had asked him to move but he wouldn't. He just said, "We've managed this long in camp, we can stay a few more months. This isn't necessary."

"Well it is for me," I said, "you can stay if you want to." The next thing I saw was Larry. "Shift over there," he said to the soldier, "before I strangle you." And with that, he pushed him out of the way. I remember thinking to myself, I've got someone with me, somebody tough with me, supporting me. And moving that little bit closer to the door, it became easier. I managed to squeeze the flattened pipe into the twisted wire. It was touch and go and I'd cut nearly halfway through my little pipe before the wire snapped, but as soon as it did, I felt the rush of fear and excitement and immediately pushed the door open. All the time I could hear the Germans next door, laughing their heads off and talking. Larry was ready and he went quickly. Mickey was next. He handed me my tunic and pack and he was off as well. The train was probably going about 30 miles per hour so I didn't want to delay too long. There was only a bit of moonlight so it was impossible to see where to jump but even so I worried that the Germans might have seen the others.

As I went down I twisted and rolled but I didn't clear the gravel, and because I hadn't fastened the sleeves of my tunic, I grazed the skin of my arm. I began to walk back following the railway line and before long found Mickey. He had rolled down from the train into some brambles so was in a bit of a bad way. We didn't stop long because we wanted to get back to Larry as soon as possible. It was quite a walk, further than between Mickey and me, but we eventually found him, sitting there waiting for us. "Christ," he said. "I thought you weren't coming. I was just wondering what to do."

We didn't really know where we were except that the next stop for the train was Ancona. I had my compass, but I was shaking so much it was impossible to use.  We were all shaking, and the only solution was for me to hold the compass on the railway line while the others held my arms to stop them from trembling.  Eventually we managed to see which way was south and set off.

A few barking dogs didn't help our nerves, but we soon found our way to the road. There we spotted the white lines on the side of a bridge and realised we would have to cross it.  We got within 100 yards before a German convoy, coming in the opposite direction, forced us to scramble down the bank of the river and into the water.  There was a bit of a splash and the water was up above our knees but we managed to get to the opposite bank unseen and, with our boots sloshing with water, carried on up a steep hill.  By the time we got to the top we'd had enough so we stopped. Within five minutes Mick and Larry were snoring, but on that first night of freedom, I couldn't sleep.

I spent much of that night planning. My uniform would give me away, but as soon as I could get some other clothes, I knew I could pretend to be Italian. For Larry and Mickey it wouldn't be so easy, they were both fair and looked very English. We had no idea how long it would take to reach the allied lines, no idea how far they were. But we knew they were there, someone had made a radio in the camp, and we knew the allies had landed. We would just take our time, get rest and food where we could, and above all, avoid recapture.

## To Pescara

In the morning we had to pick the brambles out of Mickey's skin; he was covered in them and couldn't see to take them out. We then ate some of our rations and debated where to go. Larry suggested that we should remain hidden in the shrubbery during the day and then continue walking during the night. So for the first few days that's what we did. We would walk under cover of darkness and then in the early morning we would find a place to hide, usually in some shrubbery out of the way. Within a couple of days we were on the hill overlooking our Macerata camp. We dodged round the side of that - we didn't want to go back there. Another night we ran into a vineyard and had a feast of grapes. That didn't suit Mick's stomach at all and the next day was so bad he thought he was going to die.

After about six or seven nights, we decided that we would need some different food. We couldn't keep going on porridge, spam and chocolate and we wanted some bread. We came upon a place where there was only one house, a little farmhouse. I think there were some chickens around and the only people we could see during the day were a young woman with a young girl. We approached the house during early evening to see if they had any food to give us. We didn't want to scare them so I said, "Whatever we do, we mustn't tell them we're British."

The others pointed to me and said, "You're welcome. You knock on the door." So that's what I did, and the young woman came to the door. I asked her if she had some bread for us and she dashed back in and returned with a bowl of bread. She was shaking and I said, "What's that all about?"

"Tedesco or Inglese?" she asked.

"Inglese," I said, without thinking. That's how the truth comes out of me. The woman looked relieved and she explained that the war between Italy and the British and Americans was over. She invited us in and explained that the Germans didn't like the Italians and were ill-treating people. She said that the British had arrived in Italy through the port of Termoli and the Americans were in Italy as well. Apparently her husband had been fighting in Greece and the last she had heard of him was that he was in Albania. We didn't stay long; we ate a bit of bread and some stale cheese but we didn't eat much because we knew she didn't have a lot for herself and her daughter. I think it was there that I was given a shirt and a pair of linen trousers so I could get out of my uniform. Larry and Mick managed to get some other clothes later on.

On another occasion we called at a place where we saw someone we thought was a farmer. I suggested to Mick that he should approach him. I said, "Rub your belly and say *fame* and *pane*." Mick and Larry were still in uniform at this point. The farmer shook his head, however, as if he didn't understand and tried to speak to Larry. Larry couldn't understand so the farmer approached me. I was leaning by a tree playing with a stick. I pretended that I didn't understand either. So off he went and called his son. He said, "Go quickly and tell the Germans while I give them something to eat." The son was reluctant to go on his own so a younger son was called as well.  He was equally reluctant and the two boys set off slowly.  The farmer called to them to hurry and I said to Larry, "You know where they're going?  To tell the Germans."

Larry got hold of the farmer by the neck and I said to him, "You call them back."  I was pretending I had a gun and I said, "I would shoot you but I'll leave that to someone else.  I feel sorry for those kids."  He went white.

We carried on like that, looking here and there to see if we could get a bit of bread.  And eventually, one day we met some people in the road.  There were two men in a barrel jumping up and down bashing grapes for wine.  There were also two women there. One said, "*Dove stai andando*?"  We didn't understand it at first but she wanted to know where we were going.  I said,

"England," and she laughed. I asked her if she had any food and she said, "No, we've got no food." But the other woman offered us a rabbit if we were willing to cook it. We agreed, but when the rabbit arrived it was still alive.

So we carried the rabbit with us for a while, until we came upon an isolated bungalow where we thought there might be a chance to cook it. Inside there were three women and two men. The women, they were delightful, very friendly, but the men were a little sour. One of the women was sewing; she had some black material and I think she was making a dress for herself or her mother. I told her that I could sew and they let me try the machine. With some scraps of material I made a little bag to keep my compass in. One of the men seemed to be getting a bit fed up, but Larry ignored him and went with the mother to make some porridge for us.  Eventually the mother came out and said, "Would you mind if I cook you something instead of the rabbit?"  We said we didn't mind, and she cooked us a meal.

After we had eaten I wanted to leave straight away, but I made the mistake of telling Larry that the men were talking about giving us up. "Christ," he said, "I'm not going now.  We're staying here tonight."  He wanted to keep guard all night to make sure they didn't go anywhere. We were told we could sleep in the barn so we ended up taking it in turns to watch and make sure that none of the men left during the night. I remember that I wasn't happy about this because it would have been better to get away at night and I didn't think they would have turned us in.

We left in the morning and continued on our way. We were wondering where we were going to spend the night when we spotted some Americans parachuting down not very far from us. We waited until the next morning before approaching them. They gave us some food and cigarettes and one told us that we should go to Pescara because there was to be a boat coming in on even days of the month to pick up evacuees. I'm not sure what the Americans were doing there but it is possible that they were in radio contact with others in the area. The day we met them was an 'even day', which meant we had two days to get to Pescara.

The Americans had explained that a Captain Lee would be at Pescara Bridge and we should make contact with him. We made Pescara in time but it was beginning to get dark as we arrived. We went around whispering, "Captain Lee, Captain Lee," into the night, and eventually he replied. He was quite a nice chap; he had two commandos with him and he made us welcome. He told us that he was in contact with Tito, leader of the Yugoslavian resistance movement. He gave us something to eat, and explained that the boat wasn't due for another two days. He suggested we find something to do and come back two nights later.

The next day we met a farmer who was going to pick grapes. We asked if he had anything to give us to eat. He gave us some bread and said, "You're welcome to come and pick grapes with us. Then you can come and have some dinner tonight." So that's what we did. We ended up having nearly a week there because the boat was late. We didn't do too badly. During the day we picked grapes and at night we would eat well before sleeping in a barn, ready for a good breakfast before going out to pick grapes again.

Captain Lee said eventually that he'd heard Montgomery was to be landing where we were, in Pescara, and that we should get out to avoid getting caught up in the attack. Lee decided that he would go out that night with a torch and signal out to sea. By that time there was a French Captain with a platoon of soldiers also waiting to get away. He spoke good English and told me they'd had some skirmishes with the Germans, but had been forced to stop fighting by lack of ammunition, "If all fails and the Germans come, I can only fire one magazine of the Bren and then we'll all have to disappear." They also told us there were many nationalities behind the German lines: Indians, South Africans, French,

British, Americans, Yugoslavs, Canadians, New Zealanders, Polish, Greeks and possibly more.

That night we decided to go halfway up the hill to watch Captain Lee and the two commanders signalling out to sea. We spotted a boat coming in and started walking down, but suddenly there was a burst of the Tommy gun, next a grenade and the boat was blazing. At first we started moving away, but then decided we should find out what had happened. Either Larry or Mick went down and discovered that the boat had been German. As Captain Lee was moving to shake hands with the officer on the boat, the commanders had realized he was a German officer and had opened up. Captain Lee made a hasty retreat and by the time they reached the top of the hill, two German trucks were unloading onto the bridge.

Then we heard the Bren gun go. There were a couple of bursts of the Bren gun and I think one of the bursts was from over the river, along the trees on the bank. There were three hundred to four hundred evacuees assembled on that river waiting to get on a boat and the Bren gun fire was to warn them to get away. I never did find out what happened to them all. Before we parted, Captain Lee explained why he'd taken the risk of signalling with a torch: "It's an army major in charge of the boat and I know he can't navigate because he dropped us a mile from here when he brought us up."

We decided then that it wasn't worth waiting any longer.

## To Vasto

After giving up on Captain Lee, I knew that to keep sane I had to keep going. The Italians were mostly good people. We had to watch out for the few fascists but most Italians didn't ask any questions. But there was no question of waiting for the war to end or even for the Allies to free Italy. We had to keep going.

Before we left we went to see the farmer to say goodbye and thank him for helping us. By that time I had a wound on my foot. It was caused because I'd only my old boots and they were worn out. I had been bathing the wound in seawater to stop it smelling and keep infections away. I explained to Larry and Mick that I would have to travel along the coast so that I could bathe my foot in the Adriatic. I said, "It's up to you, you can come with me through the Adriatic or you can go your own way, but I have to save my foot."

Neither Larry nor Mick knew Italian. I had learnt a little whilst in the camps, in Capua by speaking to one of the guards and in Macerata from an English prisoner who gave lessons to any of us who were interested. So they had relied on me to a certain extent to tell them what was going on. But they decided it would be easier to hide if they were away from the coast and I couldn't argue with that, so we wished each other luck and then parted.

So Larry and Mick went on inland and I followed the coastline, bathing frequently in the Adriatic. It wasn't so much fun travelling on my own. I was a bit lonely at first but soon enjoyed the freedom to do as I liked without having to persuade anyone. I had always been a bit of a loner anyway. I figured that with my dark colouring I could pass as an Italian, at least where the Germans were concerned. Both Larry and Mick had fairer skins so it would probably be harder for them, but even so, I thought they'd get through.

I continued on my way, experiencing the same problems finding food and water. I would drink from clean looking streams and I once took some water from a well with a bucket, but I was worried I'd be spotted. The Italians didn't seem to have much food themselves. I remember one house I called at, there was a woman in tears because the Germans had just called and taken the food she had for her children. Another time I was about to call at a farm when I spotted a

German truck so I stayed out of the way. Then I heard a pig squealing and saw the Germans bundling the pig into the truck. I called at the farm after the Germans had gone. I asked the farmer, "Did they pay you for the pig?" The farmer replied, "They said Mussolini would pay me."

I was constantly on the lookout for Germans and tried not to draw attention to myself because the only identification papers I had were British. As I had thought, from my appearance I could pass as an Italian and this helped. All the time I tried to take note of what the Germans were doing and where they were digging in. And if I came across any cables that could have been for German communication I would work on them with stones until they broke. The cables proved useful as a warning of where the

Germans might be.

It wasn't always possible to stay close to the coast as there were points where the Germans were digging trenches and building up defences and weaponry. One area where I was forced to go inland was the Sangro Valley. This is the valley along which the Sangro River flows east towards the Adriatic. It is a wide flat valley with a ridge to the north and another to the south. I saw the Germans building up a defensive line on the northern ridge and noted that the two bridges closest to the sea—a road bridge and a rail bridge—had been blown up. I made my way to a third bridge, which was still intact, and decided to attempt to cross here. The only alternative would have been to go much further inland, which would have delayed me a great deal. Fortunately the Germans were too busy with the work they were doing to pay much attention to a civilian crossing the bridge and I crossed without challenge.

Eventually I found myself in Vasto and reached the railway, where I found the Germans had a headquarters. On the sea side there was a big vineyard so I went through, pretending to admire the grapes whilst getting a good view of the railway. Then I come across a shed, and when I listened outside realized there were people talking in Italian. It was only a small party in there and I made myself known. They told me that there had been a group of about forty people with the same idea as me, trying to get through the German lines by going through the sea by night. But some had been seen and shot or captured, and now there were only the five of them left, three Italians and two

Yugoslavs. They had given up on the idea of going through the sea, but I still thought that I might be able to make it.

I decided to stay awhile there with the two Yugoslavs and the Italians. A farmer would come to give us spaghetti now and again. During that time I also came across three British officers who were on the run like me. When I found them in the woods they were very hungry. One was in a bad way; while I was there he pulled a big tapeworm out of his trousers. I remember thinking that the tapeworm must have left his body because there was no food left for it. I told them that I knew a farmer who might let them have some spaghetti and the farmer did oblige so they had a meal before going on their way.

One day the group I was with found an empty

bungalow and we broke in. We managed to get in through a window and then opened the door from the inside. There were frying pans and other kitchen utensils but no food. I noticed that there were cows nearby, though. They would move backwards and forwards whenever they heard guns firing. I said to the Yugoslavs, "The Italians have done enough damage in Yugoslavia. Why don't you get them to kill some of those cows and we can have a bit of fried liver?" I felt that liver was the only meat that my stomach would take by this time. So the Yugoslavs put the suggestion to the Italians and shortly afterwards I saw that the Italians had some axes. They managed to kill a cow as it was going through a small ravine close to the bungalow. Two Italians positioned themselves on opposite sides of the ravine, waiting for the cows to come by. They succeeded in slaughtering one by chopping its head off. They then chopped the carcass into smaller pieces and put them into a basket to sell in the village. They tried to exchange it for other types of food like bread, macaroni, spaghetti and salt, but there was not a lot of food around so often we were given money instead. We did get a bit of spaghetti and decided to cook some to have with our fried liver. We couldn't get any salt, so I went to the sea to get water. The spaghetti tasted like seaweed, but we got used to the taste. One of the Yugoslavs was the cook and the younger one helped him. The Italians would sell the meat in town and I was the cashier and lookout man. We managed quite well for a while. Once the meat was sold, the Italians would kill another cow and continue like that.

We did manage to make a few lire for ourselves from selling the beef and, as I was the cashier, it fell to me to divide up the money. One of the Yugoslavs was a communist and said I should divide it like Stalin and not like King George. When I asked what he meant, he explained that Stalin would say, "One for you, one for me," but King George would say, "One for you, two for me." But there was little to argue about, because there was so very little to spend the money on.

During the day my job was to be in the front room of the bungalow facing the German positions so I could keep an eye out for the enemy. But there were strings of tobacco hanging up on the wall and on one occasion I'd rolled up some of the tobacco to make a nice cigar. It was difficult to light so I had a piece of coal to keep lighting it. I wasn't concentrating on my lookout task and suddenly the door opened. I thought it was one of the Yugoslavs coming to speak to me but, instead, it was a German soldier. He didn't say a word but just marched in, picked up a chair, swung it round his shoulder and walked off with it. I was so surprised I didn't say a thing, but one of the Yugoslavs came running in to see me. "Tedesko?" he asked, and I replied, "Yeah, Tedesko."

"Didn't you see him coming?" he asked and I had to admit that I hadn't. I was laughing. I said, "He took your chair and he didn't say thank you." The Yugoslav was mad, and he told the others: "He just watched him, watched the German come and take the chair." So I said, "Well what would you have done if I'd told you the Germans were coming? You'd have started panicking."

The Germans did seem to think that they could help themselves to what they wanted. One day I saw a very young Italian girl in a field with about 50 turkeys. Some German soldiers moved her away from the turkeys and then opened up the machine gun on them. The dead birds were carried off to make a meal for the Germans.

All this time, we were only about three or four hundred yards from the Germans and I think it was probably an advantage being so close, as we could keep an eye on things. One day, I thought I'd go and wash myself a bit. It was a lovely hot day and we hadn't had a bit of water for weeks or more so I thought I'd get into the sea. There was a little embankment so I went in behind it and got into the water. I didn't take my clothes off, just left them on to clean them at the same time. I got plenty of sand and rubbed my body and my clothes with it. Then I rinsed myself in the seawater. And when I stood up in the water I saw two German soldiers smoking on top of the embankment. I didn't know what to do, but the only real option was to brazen it out. I couldn't try to dodge them. So I shook myself off like a dog and went up to the Germans, saying, "Cigarette, Senor, cigarette?" One of the Germans took out a cigarette and offered it to me trying to put it in my mouth. I was shaking so much that I bent towards the other one to get a light. All the while I was shaking my hands as if to get the water off and hoping that they wouldn't see my hands trembling. I think it was the adrenaline having that effect. I gradually walked away with my cigarette, feeling lucky to get away.

It was a tense time. The Allies sent destroyers to attack the German positions, and the railway was a particular target. German tanks were at the top of the hill above Vasto, and guns were brought into a square in the middle of Vasto to fire back at the destroyers. The Germans knew they were safe there because the Allies wouldn't shell the middle of a town.

Once, we were near the railway when some shelling was going on and we went under a railway bridge for safety. Shortly afterwards we were joined by some German soldiers who obviously had the same idea. When I saw them I started to leave, slowly making my way to the exit. I managed to get away but the rest of the group was rounded up once the danger was over and made to work, clearing up after the shelling.

I never really doubted that I would get through

the German lines, but as time went by, I was beginning to get desperate. I could never feel happy on the run, but I suppose I acclimatised myself to the situation I was in, to the potential dangers, and tried to keep my wits about me and keep scheming. I didn't really have a lot of time to think and reflect on things because I was constantly sorting myself out. There was always something; I would spend hours using my compass pin to pick out bits of corn that were embedded in my feet. Then I would head for the sea to bathe my feet in the salty water.

I decided to make an attempt by sea and talked to one of the Italians in our group, Mario, and managed to persuade him to come with me. We waited three days for a really dark evening and then went down towards the shore. We got to the last tree and from there it was sand. By this time we could hear Germans talking and laughing. We couldn't tell exactly where the voices were coming from but they seemed to be coming from a trench somewhere on the beach. I said to Mario, "If we go further down and get into the water it will be all right." But Mario insisted that we go back. I said, "No, we're going now," but suddenly I heard somebody say, "Why don't you listen to Mario and go back?" I looked around wondering who it was, but there was nobody there. The voice must have been in my head but it seemed very real. I was so startled that I agreed to go back with Mario. (I'd had a similar experience once before when travelling on my own. I had come across a fork in the road and decided to go to the right thinking it might be a short cut to the sea. A voice told me to turn and go the other way. I found out later that, had

I continued on the first path, I would have walked straight into the Germans.)

When we got back, I was still desperate enough to try again, and so asked Mario if I could borrow his identity card. Mario had another because he had been in the navy, but he was worried all the same. He agreed, but I remember him warning, "If you get caught don't tell them that I gave it to you because they will kill my family." I gave him my word, and he gave me his card.

The next day, armed with Mario's identity card and a stick, I started walking on the road. Ahead I could see the bridge that separated the Germans from the British. I thought, "Just another few hundred yards and I'll be on the other side". Then an officer jumped out and started waving a pistol, saying, "Komme.

Komme." There was nothing I could do; I had to go with him. He asked for my "documento", and I showed him Mario's identity card. I don't remember if there was a photograph on the card, but I remember the German looking carefully at it, and then at me, before eventually returning it.

I was taken to a trench where there were two Germans, was handed a shovel and told, "Arbeit!" I soon discovered that it means 'work'. So there I was, stuck in a trench, digging with two Germans. At about midnight the officer come back, jumped into the trench and started giving instructions to the two Germans. When the officer left, they started digging like mad. I was tired and said to one, tapping my head, "Malato?"

"No," he said, "Ufficiale, malato." I discovered

that if we didn't dig the trench five foot deep by five o'clock the next morning they would shoot the three of us. This was conveyed to me mostly with sign language: a hand held up indicating five and a finger pointing down, then five again and a tap on a wrist to indicate the time five o'clock. A hand making the shape of a gun pointing to each of us in turn and the word "kaput" completed the message.    The German was complaining that the night before he'd been on duty in a machine gun post and I realised he might have been one of the Germans that Mario and I had heard talking and laughing.    He complained that he hadn't had any sleep and I thought, "Yeah, you and me both."    There was nothing for it but to get through the night working with blisters on my hands. I didn't really believe the officer was going to shoot us until the next morning at about five or six o'clock when he came with a tape.

My heart was pounding as the officer proceeded to measure the depth of the trench. Fortunately, it was deep enough and the officer was satisfied. He then called me and said, "Now you go back." He pointed across the river and told me the English and Americans were over there, he told me to go back and not to come again, because if I came through at night I'd be shot. And if I came through by day, I'd be working again.

At that I went back to find Mario. I had been so long, he thought I'd got through, but I showed him the blisters on my hands and told him what I'd been doing all night.

That day I slept, but was woken by a woman who came along and kicked at my feet, saying,

"Americanos, Americanos." I listened and heard a machine gun firing. For me there was no mistaking the sound of the Bren, and I told her, "No, not the Americans—it's Inglese."

It seemed as if a battle was imminent. Shortly afterwards I was between a machine gunner down by the railway and the little shed where I went to make my cigars. A soldier came and said, "You have to go back; if you come any further forward, I'm going to shoot you." I did go away, but after a while went back because I wanted to see what was going on. I got so far when I saw the soldier pick up his machine gun. There was a burst of fire and I had to jump into a ditch. The firing stopped, but I stayed there for a little while and then I crept out. I was still interested to see how the fighting was going on so I found an olive tree that I could hide in. I climbed up and found a comfortable spot with a very good view of a tank battle that was going on between the Germans and the British in a field on the other side away from the sea. There were tanks knocked out on both sides and by the evening, the battle stopped. I wondered what was going on, but then I saw soldiers coming from the direction of the trench that I'd helped to dig and they seemed to be moving out. I went down to see where they were going, and followed them up the hill and away from Vasto. It was clear that they were leaving.

I then went back to the bridge where the Germans had been, but by the time I got there it was late. Allied soldiers would be on guard, and if they were a bit jumpy, they could pull a trigger on me. So I decided to wait until the morning. I lay there and struggled to sleep—it was cold and there was still some shelling. The next morning I walked over the bridge and when the British soldiers spotted me—there were only two—they told me to put my hands up. After I told them that I was a British soldier, they still insisted I put my hands up, so I did that and approached. I managed to persuade them that I'd left my AB64 behind and I had to go and get it. I also asked to see their officer. By that time they were convinced and they brought me food and cigarettes. But I absolutely didn't want to eat anything. I didn't think my stomach would take it. I had a cigarette and that went to my head. At last I was back with the British Army. It felt as though I'd drunk a whole bottle of whiskey.

I knew I had made it when I first saw the Germans leaving Vasto. But it was only when I was talking to our chaps at last and getting something eat that I felt completely safe. By this time it was early November and it was beginning to get quite cold. I really don't know how I would have managed if I had been on the run through the winter months.

During my time on the run, though, I had acquired a good deal of information about the German activities. I immediately suggested to the platoon commander that he could get his troops to stand down because the Germans had gone. "Oh," he said, "I think you'd better speak to our company commander." When I saw him, he said, "We've just been waiting for the tanks to come up to go into Vasto this morning and they haven't turned up." I told him, "I think they lost quite a few yesterday. They had quite a big battle over there." He sent for an officer—I think he was a captain—to go into Vasto with the Bren carriers. The officer was worried. He said, "You know the Bren carriers don't you?" I said I did. So he said, "You know it only needs one grenade and they're finished." I said, "Now don't worry, there's nobody there, they're all gone. I'll come with you because I have to get my AB64 that I buried there."

After I'd picked up my ID, I turned to go back and he said, "By the time you get back there, you shall hear our destiny." I said again, "Don't worry, everything is going to be okay." And not long after I got back a message came through on the radio and the company commander announced, "Vasto is in our hands." Everybody cheered.

Later I was told that there was an officer who was interested to hear what intelligence I had.

During the debriefing, the officer told me that Montgomery wanted to get to Pescara in four days. I remember saying, "Well, you ought to tell General Montgomery that if he wants to get to Pescara in four days he'll need to make a quick landing because going by land he won't get there in four months. "What, what?" the officer said.

I asked him to get a map so I could explain. I pointed out the Sangro Valley and told him all I knew about the German preparations on the northern ridge. I emphasised how exposed an army would be if an attempt was made to cross the valley as there was no cover for about a quarter of a mile each side of the river. I was also able to show him the bridge I had used and also explain exactly where the bridge was wired up on the western side in readiness for demolition when the Germans withdrew. I thought that somebody approaching the bridge covertly from inland under cover of darkness would be able to make the bridge safe. I had seen all this on my journey from Pescara. As I went through the bridge I had leaned over and seen the wire and seen where they were put the explosives."

After the debriefing I was told that if I went to the road I might find some engineers and get a lift to Termoli. On the way to the road the first troops I saw were from an Indian division. They were sitting around and as I approached they mistook me for an Italian and started shouting, "Vai, vai," as they waved their guns at me. I said, "Can anybody speak English? Anybody speak English?" and eventually a sergeant appeared "Yes," he said, "I can speak English." He said, "I'm an escapee British soldier myself." I explained, "I'm making my way back to Termoli but it seems the Indians don't like the Italians." He agreed, and I said, "Well, you know, the Italians, they don't like you? They reckon you're pinching their chickens." That made him laugh and he walked me to the road, chatting.

From there I made my way down to the bridge where the engineers were putting up a new bridge. The officer there was friendly and he said, "We've got no transport here but sometimes there is something going by and you might have a bit of luck. You might not have to wait long." I was very scruffy by this time; I hadn't been able to shave or get my haircut for a long time and I had no shoes; my old ones had worn out on the journey from Pescara. The wound on my foot had healed, but I had more damage to the soles of my feet caused by walking barefoot through cornfields. The officer suggested that I should wait by a puddle in the road, as the trucks would have to slow down there, and I could push my AB64 under the driver's nose. This was necessary as the Italians had been making a bit of a nuisance of themselves trying to get transported everywhere.

## Termoli, Taranto and Home

The plan worked well and I was soon on my way to Termoli, and once there to a barber to shave my beard and cut my hair. I was frightened to look in the mirror until it was done, so I shut my eyes until the barber had finished. At Termoli I saw one of the officers that I'd met in the woods around Vasto. I was also summoned by the Corps Commander for another debriefing.

Again I recounted what I knew and the Corps Commander seemed satisfied with what I told him. There were no clothes or boots available for me in Termoli so I had to wait until I reached Taranto.

We set off for Taranto later that day and arrived at night. When I said that I was in the 5$^{th}$ Hampshire regiment I was told to wait, as Colonel Newnham had given orders that he be told if any of us turned up, even if he was asleep. The Colonel appeared in his pyjamas and put his arms round me. I still remember his smile and his words of greeting, "My little rogue! My little rogue!"

There were many at Taranto waiting to get back to England. Many of them were experienced officers who were going back to prepare for action in France. Eventually we were put on a boat heading for Algiers and from there we joined the boat that was to take us home.

*** 

Thinking back on all this convinces me that I did the right thing when I escaped. Yes, it was hard, what with the constant gnawing indigestion, the exhaustion, the holes in my feet from walking barefoot through cornfields, and the fact that I always needed to be alert. I would never know what was round the corner, and it meant that for months on end I could never properly relax.

During the battle at Sidi Nsir there was a brief moment when I wished no-one in the world knew me, so that nobody would be sad if I didn't get home. And as soon as I was captured I knew that I had to escape. From then on my mind was taken over by plans and preparations. And thinking back I remember the determination all three of us had to make it home, as we stood there shaking with nerves by the railway track, having jumped from the train.

The one thing I don't know how to explain are the voices that I heard at those moments of danger. Some might talk about guardian angels but I don't believe in fairies, so the voices must have been entirely in my head. Whatever their source, I just know I am grateful for them.

## Post Script

After arriving safely back in England I was eventually sent to the Eastern Command, firstly in Luton Hoo and then in Hounslow. I was once again given the task of cutting hair. This was considered to be a light duty; I had been put on light duties for six months because I wasn't one hundred percent fit. I had lost a lot of weight and found it difficult to eat rich foods. The hair dressing proved interesting to me because I came into contact with officers, including General Kenneth Anderson, who had been in charge in Tunisia whilst I was there. I was summoned to his battle room in Luton Hoo to cut his hair. My impression was of a very kind man. He questioned me about my war experiences and referred to the maps on the walls as he discussed what was currently going on. Other officers also kept me informed. One told me that the British had taken even longer to reach Pescara than I had estimated. I was also happy to hear that the bridge across the Sangro River had been made safe by soldiers from an Indian regiment. I wondered whether those soldiers had been among those I had met in Vasto.

*By 5th November 1943, Vasto was in the hands of the British as the 76th Panzer Corps, under the command of General Herr, was forced to concede ground. The British 8th Army, under the command of General Montgomery, was then preparing to advance up the east coast of Italy to the 'Rome Line' which extended from Rome, through Avezzano in the mountains, to Pescara on the coast. Bad weather and a forced delay to allow for the building up of supplies for Montgomery, afforded extra time for the Germans to strengthen their considerable defences.*

*The 8th Army's first main objective was to reach the port of Ortona by 20th November. By this date, however, the 8th Army had only just succeeded the crossing the Sangro River. This had proved to be a mighty challenge. Later the whole offensive proved very costly and supplies were running so low that on the 27th December, Montgomery called a halt on the Ortona/Orsogna line. On the 31ˢᵗ December General Montgomery returned to Britain to take up command of the 21ˢᵗ Army Group, handing over command of the 8ᵗʰ Army to General Leese.*

*The Allies finally took Pescara on 10ᵗʰ June 1944.*

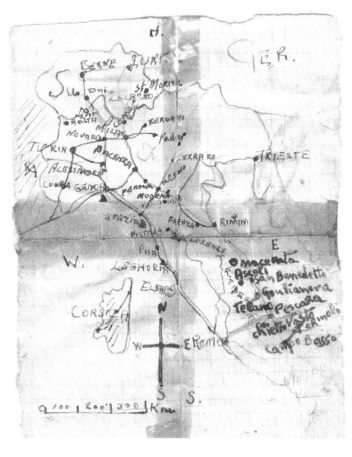

*Figure 1 My Map of Italy Sketched in Capua POW Camp*

*Figure 2. Compass given to me by an RAF Sergeant in Macerata POW Camp*

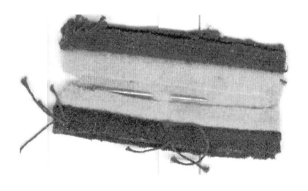

*Figure 3. My company ribbon complete with pin to hold my compass*

Printed in Great Britain
by Amazon

76225170R00066